The Miracle In the Cave: The Incredible Story of 13 Soccer Kids' Survival

INTRODUCTION

The story is about 13 young soccer players who, while exploring a cave in their hometown, become trapped deep within its depths. With no way to call for help and no food or water, the boys must use all of their strength, resilience, and teamwork to survive in the cave for over 30 days.

As the days go on, the boys face numerous challenges and obstacles, including hunger, dehydration, and darkness. They must work together to find sources of water, ration their dwindling food supplies, and keep each other's spirits up in the face of immense danger.

The world watches with bated breath as rescuers work tirelessly to free the boys, and the boys themselves never give up hope, even in the darkest of moments. In the end, against all odds, all 13 of the boys are rescued and reunited with their families, inspiring people around the world with their incredible resilience and strength of spirit

CONTENTS

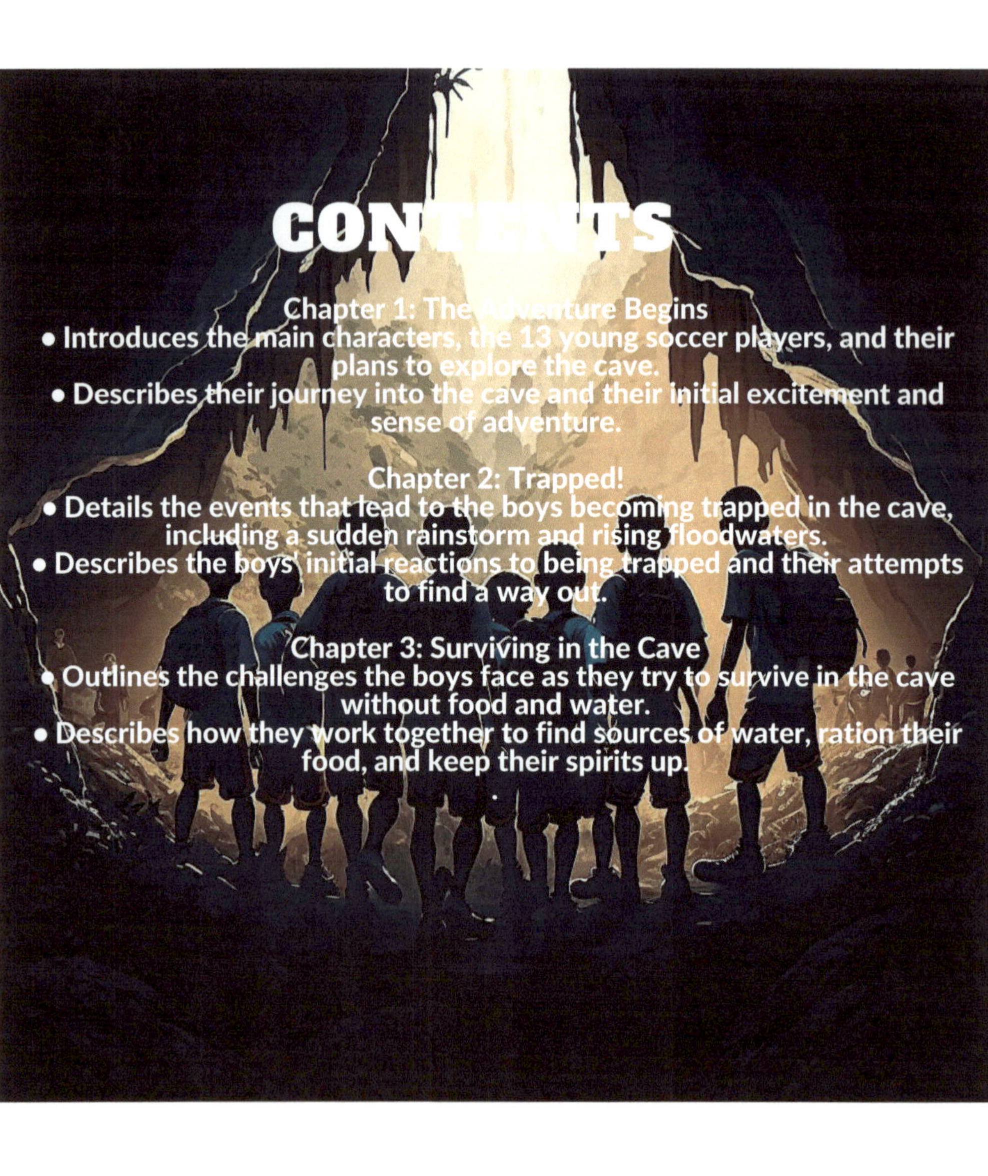

CONTENTS

Chapter 4: Searching for a Way Out
- Details the efforts of rescue workers and volunteers to locate and rescue the boys.
- Describes the various strategies used to try and reach the boys and bring them to safety.

Chapter 5: Maintaining Hope
- Details the emotional toll of being trapped in the cave and the boys' struggles to maintain hope and stay positive.
- https://s.mj.run/rkNyDhr-3GM
- Describes the support the boys receive from their families and the global community.

Chapter 6: The Final Push
- Details the successful rescue of the boys and their reunion with their families.
- Describes the emotions the boys and their families experience and the incredible resilience and strength of spirit that enabled the boys to survive.

Chapter 7: Reflection and Gratitude
- Offers a reflection on the events of the story and the lessons that can be learned from the boys' survival.
- Expresses gratitude for the hard work of the rescue workers, the support of the global community, and the bravery and strength of the 13 young soccer players

Deep in the heart of a jungle town
A team of young soccer stars, all renowned
Set out to explore a cave, hidden away
To play and adventure, to laugh and to play

With helmets and flashlights, they entered the cave
Excited and fearless, ready to be brave
Step by step, they made their way in
And the deeper they went, the more they grinned

As they passed through tunnels, narrow and tight
The boys felt their spirits take flight
The thrill of adventure, the joy of the game
All of it was there, with no one to blame

In the heart of the cave, they found a big room
And the boys shouted out in joy and in gloom
For they saw what they came for, a perfect space
To play soccer, to have fun, to embrace

And so the adventure began, deep in the cave
With a ball at their feet, they played to their heart's crave
Kicking and laughing, they lost track of time
As they reveled in the game, under the cave's shine

But little did they know, that adventure awaits
For something unexpected, the cave has in store for their fate
And so the boys played on, unaware of the storm
And what was to come, in the cave's deadly form

The rain came down in sheets so thick,
It pounded the roof, it made the cave sick.
The boys played on, they didn't care,
But the water rose, and it was a scare.

They tried to leave, they tried to run,
But the water blocked them, it wasn't fun.
They shouted for help, but no one came,
And soon they realized, they were trapped in the game.

They huddled together, in a tight embrace,
Their smiles turned to frowns, on their face.
The darkness closed in, they couldn't see,
And their hearts sank, as they thought of their family.

They searched for a way out, they tried to climb,
But the walls were too slick, it was a waste of time.
Their stomachs growled, their throats went dry,
And they knew that survival, was the only way to fly.

They huddled for warmth, they tried to rest,
But the cave was so cold, it put them to the test.
They clung to each other, for strength and for might,
And prayed to be rescued, before the end of the night.

The water kept rising, they couldn't escape,
And the boys were forced, to confront their own fate.
But they held on, with all of their heart,
And vowed to survive, and not to fall apart.

The boys were trapped, but not alone,
They had each other, they had grown.
Together they faced, the challenge ahead,
To survive the cave, without being dead.

They searched for water, they searched for food,
And found a way, to lift their mood.
With teamwork and courage, they pressed on,
And showed the world, how to stay strong.

They rationed their food, they rationed their drink,
And prayed that soon, they would be in sync.
The cave was dark, but their spirits shone bright,
As they fought for survival, day and night.

The days turned to weeks, the weeks to a month,
And the boys endured, with a fierce resolve.
They knew that rescue, was their only hope,
And so they clung to life, with all their might.

The cave was their home, the boys its guests,
And they showed the world, how to be their best.
For in the face of danger, they did not falter,
But instead, they rose up, like a shining altar.

And when the rescue finally came,
The boys emerged, from their cave of pain.
They had survived, against all odds,
And shown the world, what it means to be a squad.

The boys were saved, but still not free,
For they had to find a way, out of the cave's debris.
The rescue team arrived, with hope in their hearts,
But the boys knew that the journey, was just about to start.

They followed the rescuers, through the twists and turns,
Their hearts were filled with hope, as the torches burned.
They climbed and they crawled, with all their might,
And kept pushing forward, into the night.

The journey was tough, but they never gave up,
For they knew that the way out, was their only hope,
They searched for signs, for clues and for light,
And held on tight, with all of their might.

The cave was dark, but the boys were strong,
And they knew that their journey, would not be too long.
For in the face of danger, they had learned to thrive,
And they knew that their survival, was their true prize.

And then, just when they thought, they could go no more,
They saw a glimmer of light, that shone from the door.
The rescue team had found it, the way out of the cave,
And the boys emerged, from their dark and lonely grave.

They hugged and they cried, as the fresh air filled their lungs,
For they had come so close, to the end of their runs.
But they had survived, with courage and grace,
And they knew that their journey, would be a story to embrace

The boys were out, they were safe and sound,
But the experience, had left a deep wound.
They knew they were lucky, to be alive,
But they couldn't help, but feel like they'd died.

The rescue team had praised them, for their strength and
their heart,
But the boys still felt, like they'd been torn apart.
They missed their families, they missed their home,
And the memories of the cave, made them feel so alone.

But they knew that they had, to keep on going,
For life was a journey, that kept on flowing.
They talked to each other, and shared their dreams,

They went back to school, to their studies and their play,
And tried to forget, the horrors of that day.
But the memories still lingered, in the back of their mind,
And they knew that they had, to leave them behind.

They played soccer, their favorite game,
And tried to remember, that life was not the same.
For they had been through, the darkest of nights,
And had emerged, with a newfound light.

They maintained their hope, for a better tomorrow,
And knew that they had, to embrace the sorrow.
For in the face of adversity, they had found their way,
And the memory of the cave, would never go away

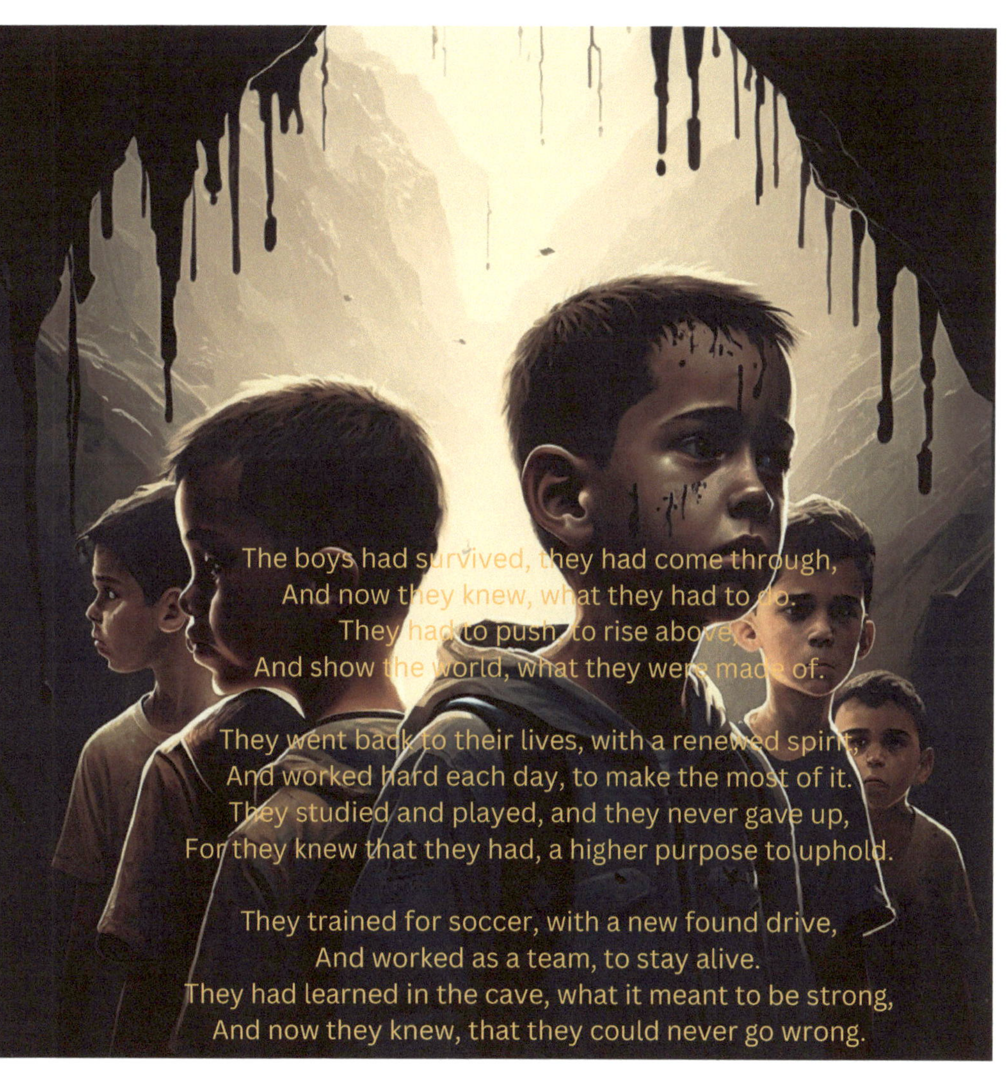

The boys had survived, they had come through,
And now they knew, what they had to do.
They had to push, to rise above,
And show the world, what they were made of.

They went back to their lives, with a renewed spirit,
And worked hard each day, to make the most of it.
They studied and played, and they never gave up,
For they knew that they had, a higher purpose to uphold.

They trained for soccer, with a new found drive,
And worked as a team, to stay alive.
They had learned in the cave, what it meant to be strong,
And now they knew, that they could never go wrong.

They faced challenges, that came their way,
And with each one, they grew stronger each day.
They had faced their worst fear, and had come out on top,
And now they knew, that they would never stop.

They inspired their friends, and the people around,
And showed them that, they could be unbound.
For they had faced death, and had come out alive,
And they knew that they had, so much more to strive.

And so they pushed on, towards a brighter future,
And knew that they had, the power to nurture.
For they had faced the darkest of days,
And now they knew, that they had found their way.

And when they played soccer, they did it with pride,
For they had learned, to never hide.
For they had been through, the final push,
And now they knew, that they could never hush.

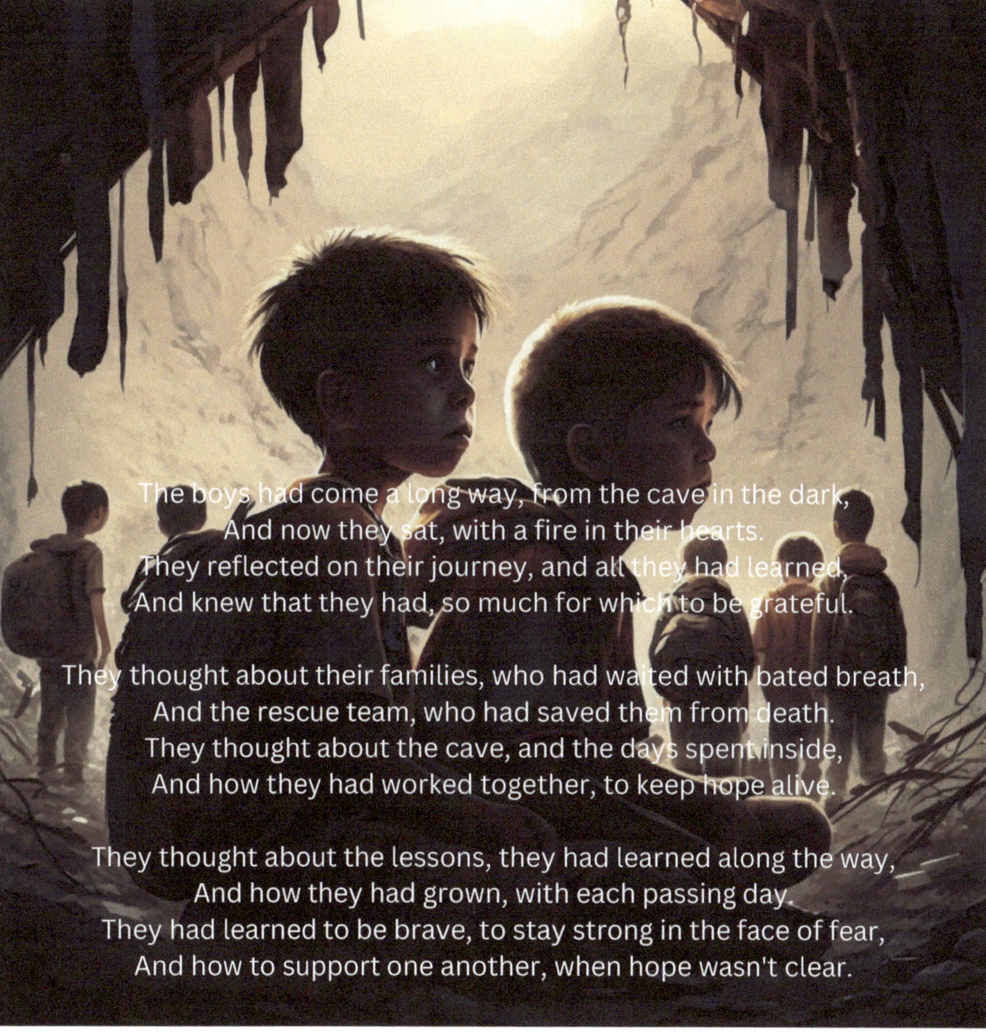

The boys had come a long way, from the cave in the dark,
And now they sat, with a fire in their hearts.
They reflected on their journey, and all they had learned,
And knew that they had, so much for which to be grateful.

They thought about their families, who had waited with bated breath,
And the rescue team, who had saved them from death.
They thought about the cave, and the days spent inside,
And how they had worked together, to keep hope alive.

They thought about the lessons, they had learned along the way,
And how they had grown, with each passing day.
They had learned to be brave, to stay strong in the face of fear,
And how to support one another, when hope wasn't clear.

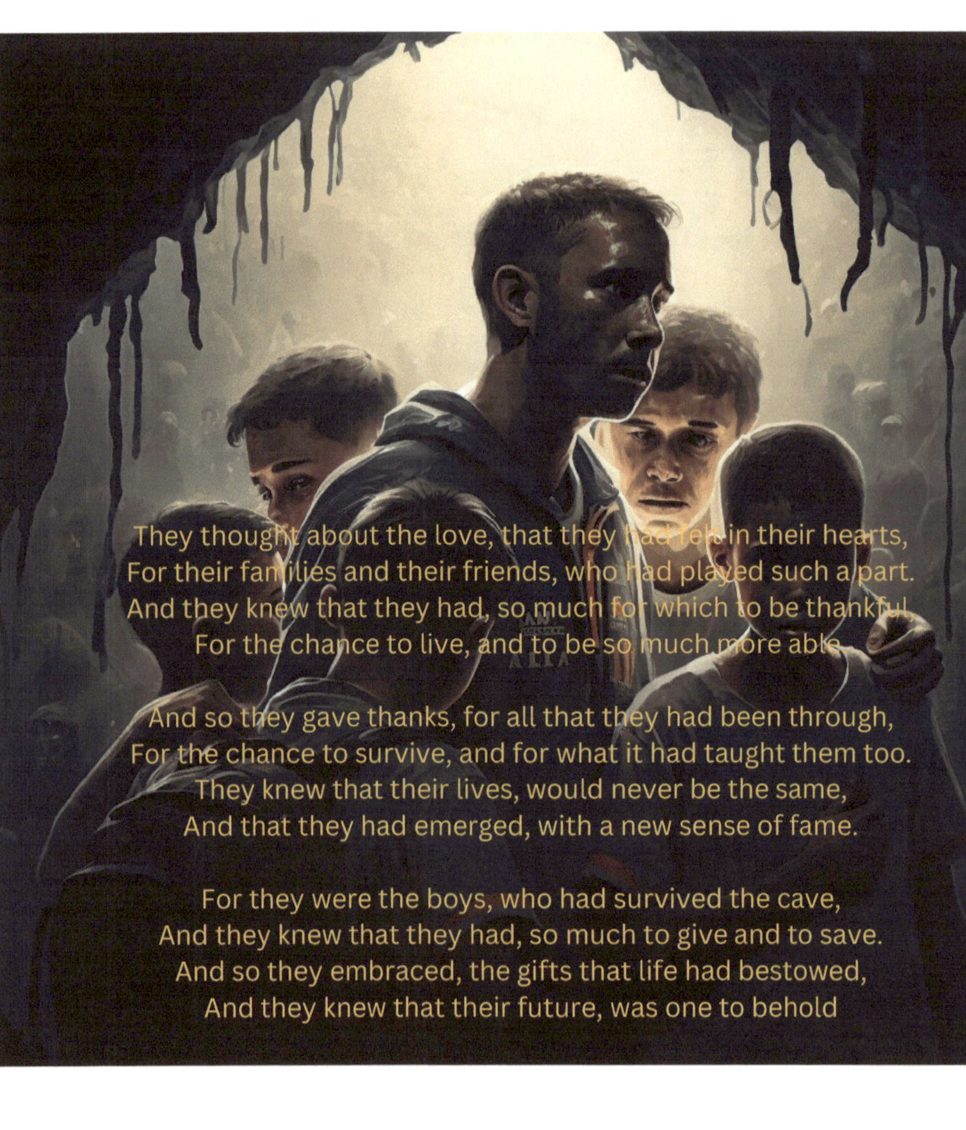

They thought about the love, that they had felt in their hearts,
For their families and their friends, who had played such a part.
And they knew that they had, so much for which to be thankful,
For the chance to live, and to be so much more able.

And so they gave thanks, for all that they had been through,
For the chance to survive, and for what it had taught them too.
They knew that their lives, would never be the same,
And that they had emerged, with a new sense of fame.

For they were the boys, who had survived the cave,
And they knew that they had, so much to give and to save.
And so they embraced, the gifts that life had bestowed,
And they knew that their future, was one to behold

END OF STORY

ABOUT THE AUTHOR

Kenshin Sadow is a passionate writer with a love for crafting stories that transport readers to new worlds and inspire them to see the world in a different light. He has been writing for over 15 years, and has honed his craft through a combination of formal education and personal experience.

His stories often explore themes of identity, family, and personal growth, and are grounded in his own experiences as a son, father, and husband. John believes in the power of storytelling to connect people from different backgrounds and cultures, and strives to create characters that readers can relate to on a deep and emotional level.

In addition to writing, John is also an avid traveler and photographer, and has visited numerous countries around the world. He draws inspiration from the people and places he encounters on his travels, and is always looking for new ways to incorporate these experiences into his writing.

Kenshin currently lives in Los Angeles with his wife and two children, and when he's not writing, he enjoys hiking in the nearby mountains and exploring the city's vibrant cultural scene.

Shark Skin Suit: Dictator Leaders of the World

Introduction:

The concept of dictatorship has been present throughout the history of human civilization. The idea of one person or a small group of people having absolute power over a nation is one that has intrigued and horrified people for centuries. In this book, we will explore the lives of some of the most notorious dictator leaders in the world, from the ancient times to the present day.

Chapter 1: Ancient Dictatorships

In this chapter, we will explore the earliest forms of dictatorships, such as the Roman Empire, ancient Greece, and the various kingdoms of Asia. We will examine the lives of rulers such as Julius Caesar, Alexander the Great, and Genghis Khan, and analyze the impact of their reigns on the civilizations they ruled over.

Chapter 2: European Dictatorships

This chapter will focus on the rise of European dictatorships in the 20th century, particularly the fascist regimes of Italy, Spain, and Germany. We will examine the lives of dictators such as Benito Mussolini and Francisco Franco, and analyze the ways in which they gained and maintained power, as well as the consequences of their regimes for their respective countries and the world at large.

Chapter 3: Communist Dictatorships

In this chapter, we will explore the rise of communist dictatorships in the 20th century, particularly in the Soviet Union and China. We will examine the lives of leaders such as Joseph Stalin and Mao Zedong, and analyze the ways in which their regimes differed from fascist dictatorships, as well as the impact of their rule on their respective countries and the world.

Chapter 4: African and Middle Eastern Dictatorships

This chapter will focus on the rise of dictators in Africa and the Middle East, from the colonial period to the present day. We will examine the lives of leaders such as Idi Amin, Muammar Gaddafi, and Saddam Hussein, and analyze the ways in which they gained and maintained power, as well as the impact of their regimes on their respective countries and the world.

Chapter 5: Modern Dictatorships

In this final chapter, we will examine the current state of dictatorship in the world, focusing on leaders such as Kim Jong-un of North Korea and Bashar al-Assad of Syria. We will analyze the ways in which these leaders have maintained their power, and the challenges they face in the modern era of globalization and technological progress.